The Three Legged Table

Why Every Employee Matters

BRIAN JAMES MBA

ISBN: 1479156612
ISBN 13: 9781479156610

Library of Congress Control Number: 2012915243
CreateSpace, Independent Publishing Platform
North Charleston, South Carolina

To my parents,
Cheryl, Vicki and Nancy

Preface
Why Every Employee Matters

In the words reported by Patricia Fripp, """Your business is as good as your worst employee".[1]

On other words, every employee has a vital role in the functioning of an organization. In fact, if an employee had no role in the organization, why would they continue to be employed?

Looking at the chain of command, the CEO is important because they have the primary responsibility of developing the best directions of the organization. The managers and supervisors are responsible for directing the day-to-day operations of their departments, line employee perform the basic functions of the organizations, whether it is in sales, health care, or any other field. Finally, there are the men and women responsible for the cleanliness and maintenance of the facility.

While the various individuals have differing levels of responsibility, each employee has an important role in the organization's operational productivity, financial performance, and how the public perceives the organization.[2] [3]

---

1 Fripp, P., Evans, B. Customer Service Is Only As Good As Your Worst Personnel. (Online). August 15, 2012. From: http://realtytimes.com/ rtpages/19981113_service.htm

2 Gallup Poll. (2010). Employee engagement: what's your engagement ratio? (Brochure.) (Online). May 13, 2011. http://www.google.com/search?sourceid=navc lient&aq=0&oq=employee+engagement+what%27s+&ie=UTF-8&rlz=1T4HPIB_en US313US313&q=employee+engagement+what%27s+your+engagement+ratio

3 Northwestern University (n.d.) Forum for People Performance and Measurement; Executive Summary: Linking organizational characteristics to

In the following pages, I discuss how each employee affects each of these areas, followed by some common pitfalls that sabotage employee morale, and finally, the importance of leaders and mentors in overcoming these pitfalls and how they boost employee morale and performance.

While I believe that the following discussions apply to most organizations, and industries, the specific points of the conversation will be related to the health care industry, and more specifically, hospitals.

This focus is related to my own personal work and educational experiences in health care, primarily in hospitals, and primarily in echocardiography (ultrasound examinations of the cardiac structures).

For illustration purposes, I will discuss how customer service in the health care industry is represented by a three legged table.

The table top represents the customers, or patients, that are being served. The floor, upon which the table sits, represents the physical facilities of the organization. In between are the three supports of the table top.

These three supports represent separate, yet vital players in providing health care.

These legs represent the role administration, the role of physicians, and the roles of the support staff.

I suspect that this same model may apply to other industries, as an example; in the restaurant industry we could substitute the roles of administration, the kitchen staff and wait staff. The administration creates schedules, and manages the work flow, the kitchen staff prepares the food to appearance and customer preferences, and the wait staff delivers the food items, the cleanliness and availability of the counters and tables.

Each plays an important role in overall performance of the operation and delivery of the food service. The actions of each team has the potential to disrupt the actions of the other members overall service team.

---

employee attitudes and behaviors: a look at the downstream effects on market response & financial performance. (Online) May 14, 2011.
http://www.incentivecentral.org/pdf/employee_engagement_study.pdf

It should be noted that while the examples in the following pages are specific, many are fictitious, and have been created for discussion purposes. The exceptions to this are the situations that identify a specific incidence.

The first chapter starts with a discussion of the importance of customer service, and introduces the idea of the delivery of customer service as a three legged table.

CHAPTER 1

THE THREE LEGS OF THE TABLE

....

Great minds discuss ideas; average minds discuss events; small minds discuss people.

ELEANOR ROOSEVELT

....

Customer service – the holy grail of every organization.

The importance of customer service is almost impossible to underestimate. It drives the need to provide goods and services, and directly affects the revenues and profits of every organization.

In almost every industry, and every organization, customer· service is so important that is measured, monitored, and reported on monthly, quarterly and yearly basis. Reports are generated for the entire organization, every divisions and each individual department. The data generated is used to evaluate performance, adjust salaries, create bonuses and make personnel decisions.

There are thousands of studies, reports, opinions, ideas and commentaries that attempt to define, isolate, and identify what creates good customer service. These same efforts also discuss how customer service affects customer retention and loyalty, and, ultimately, financial performance. Additionally, there are missives on how corporate culture and management styles affect employee satisfaction, employee burnout and retention, and the effectiveness of differing management/leadership styles.

Many of these commentaries relate that the one concept that resonates through these reports is that employee satisfaction strongly positively correlates with customer satisfaction. In most cases, these reports are generated by research and educational persons and organizations, or by an administrator that has worked for organizations that have achieved high customer satisfaction. In other words, their ideas are based either on a laboratory model, or by an individual who has demonstrated some success at improving the bottom line at a high corporate level.

Yet, despite the millions of words, paragraphs and papers that attempt to define these characteristics there is no one idea that summarizes, or identifies, that one single trait that explains how to positively affect employee satisfaction.

The goal of this paper is to introduce thinking processes that are generated from the lower levels of the corporate ladder, looking inward and upward. The following ideas and concepts that are presented have been generated from the perspective and experience of a collective of thoughts and ideas that have been generated over decades of personal experiences, education and interviews of individuals in varying levels of the organizational ladder. In order to present scientific support of these hypotheses, the aforementioned scientific reports, ideas and quotes from various professionals are presented in an effort to promote further discussion.

These ideas and concepts have been collected over decades of experience as a health care professional. With this in mind, many of the specifics of this discussion will be directed toward health care. While these comments may apply to health care organizations, many of the observations presumably apply to other industries.

Collectively, these experiences have been collected from work experiences at differing institutions, ranging from small health care facilities to world class medical institutions. They also reflect the responses of thousands of administrators, physicians, nurses, technicians and other medical personnel.

In order to provide a model for discussion, let us think of customer service as a three legged table. The table top will represent customer service and the items located on top of the table represent our customers. The physical building and equipment create the "floor" which the table sets.

Finally, the table legs represent the three primary components of the health care organization. They will be designated as the administration; the physicians; and the nurses, technicians and support staff of the company (collectively referred to as technicians).

In looking at our table, each leg must provide an equal amount of support to ensure that the table top is level and able to support a given amount of weight. That is to say that the each leg, the administration, physicians and technicians, must provide an equal amount of support in order to create an environment in which customer service is provided at a world class level.

In the event that one of these legs is weakened, the table top becomes uneven. In this event, customer support is compromised, and the table can no longer provide the level of customer support that its patients have come to expect. The result is that the performance of the organization is diminished, and this results in losing customers to competitors.

Conversely, if all of the legs are equally strengthened, then customer service is improved, the organization provides customer support, and more patients will be served by the institution.

The legs of the table, inherently, are made of individuals. Each employee is a part of one the legs of our table. The administrative team works with the team of physicians, with the team of nurses, technicians and support staff in an effort to provide care in a coordinated manner to ensure the best medical care.

In health care, the administration provides support for the patients and staff by creating an environment that is safe and effective for the customers and staff members. The physicians are the conductors of the patient care and ensure that patient is given the best possible care. The nurses, technicians and support staff work together to provide a safe and supportive environment for the patient. This includes coordinating the processes of admission, the procedure and completing the final results of the examination.

All these parties must work together to achieve the best results. Should any of these pieces falter, there are delays, the test may be incomplete, the final report may be incomplete or the medical records may not be accurate. Failings in any one of these areas will inconvenience the patient, the staff, the physician and the administration.

Given this situation, it becomes apparent that each member of the health care institution is interdependent upon each other. That is, while each branch has distinct and separate roles and responsibilities, they are dependent upon the other to provide services and support.

As an example, consider a patient making a "simple" hospital visit.

The first step is that the client calls the hospital to make an appointment. During this phone call, the receptionist gathers the patient's information and the primary reason for the appointment. The secretary then reviews a schedule and finds an appointment that is compatible with the customer's schedule. Staff and physician availability are determined by administrative and physician policy to ensure that a timely and efficient visit may be achieved.

Upon arrival at the hospital, the receptionist has the patient fill out an office form, which includes patient information, insurance coverage, associated risk factors, known allergies, and the reason for the visit. This information is collected for administrative purposes, such as billing, medical records, and patient accounting. It is also important for the physician, in order to provide information to make an accurate diagnosis and treatment plan. In addition, previous medical records are accessed so that a complete picture of the patient's medical history and medication records is achieved.

Upon arrival at the hospital the patient completes any necessary paper work; this may include billing information, a description of the reason for the clinic visit, and a brief medical history, including any known allergic reactions. Following the completion of the necessary forms, the secretary informs the physician's nurse that the patient is available. The nurse then gathers and places the patient in an examination room, collects vital signs, reaffirms the reason for the appointment, and any other information as necessary. Following this interview, the nurse enters these impressions into the patient's medical records. Once this step is completed, the nurse communicates with the physician that this initial interview is completed and that the patient is ready for consultation.

During this visit, the physician makes further notes and observations that allow them to make an accurate diagnosis, including developing a treatment plan. This treatment plan may include prescriptions, medical testing and follow-up. Information from the patient's reported allergic reactions are considered in prescribing medications or medical procedures to be prescribed.

Finally, this information is recorded in the medical record and relayed to the office nurse and technicians. Inaccurate or incomplete documentation may result in improper medications, examinations and errors in billing procedures.

In this scenario, it becomes clear that while each leg of our clinic works independently, they must also communicate and coordinate with the other parts of the organization. Each of the steps in the process play an integral part in the patient visit, whether it be related to a efficient visit, accurate collection of diagnostic information, or billing information. Any interruption or inaccurate recording results in a delay of the appointment, missing health information, or inaccurate patient and billing information. Any of the errors or lapses in communication will also in affect productivity, customer service.

The World Health Organization states that "Health is a state of complete physical, mental and social well-being and not merely the absence of disease or infirmity."[1]

The administrators, physicians, technicians, nurses and support personnel that provide care need embody this ideal. The caring, kindness and compassion that each of these individuals provides help to cure not only the broken bones and illnesses that afflict us, they also provide the gentleness, support and genuineness that heals the soul as well as the body.

This is the mission of every person that serves in health care. This responsibility extends down from the CEO of the largest hospital to the nursing assistants and housekeeping personnel.

While each individual has different levels of responsibility, each member of the health care team has an equal opportunity, either directly, or indirectly, to provide the best patient experience.

The financial performance of these organizations is necessary to keep the doors open of these same institutions. This ideal is enhanced when these same employees work in respectful and caring environments. The way that we treat the members of the health care team directly influences how these individuals perform their responsibilities and respond to their customers.

By treating employees fairly, respectfully and with compassion, they will treat their peers and patients with these same ideals and attitudes.

These behaviors and attitudes are not limited to the health care industry, but are applicable in all fields of business.

As we will discuss in later chapters, in health care or in other professions, there is often a gap between the employees, which rely on their clinical skills and knowledge, and the individuals in administration that, in many cases, have a background in business management. This gap results in communication failures that frustrate both the employee and the senior executive.

In the following pages, we will review these, and present ideas to bridge this gap.

---

1 Constitution of the World Health Organization. (Basic Documents, Forty-fifth edition, Supplement, October 2006). New York, N.Y.

Finally, in effort to provide more information, there is a combination of research, famous quotes and references for further study and review.

In the words of Eleanor Roosevelt: Great minds discuss ideas; average minds discuss events; average minds discuss people.

I hope that these works start some discussions.

CHAPTER 2

THE ROLES AND RESPONSIBILITIES
OF THE THREE LEGS

In this chapter, we will discuss the three "legs" of our table. Many of these comments may be related to other industries; however parts of the following discussion will be related directly to the health care industry.

Each of the three "legs" of our organization has different roles and responsibilities in creating customer service. Despite the separate characteristics of each section, in health care it is essential that all parts of this triad must work together seamlessly to create the highest levels of performance and service.

The interdependence of the divisions requires that all parties are working toward the same goals. The mission, vision and values of the organization must be adopted and practiced by every member of the corporate ladder. Failure to model these ideals will compromise the overall effectiveness of the organization.

Since the mission, vision and values are created at the upper levels of the administration, a discussion of their roles and actions affect the attitudes and behaviors of the front lime employee's customer service will be presented. After this initial section, the physician role will be discussed, with a final section regarding the technical staff.

Administration

The primary role of the administrative branch is ensuring the efficient operations of the organization and adherence to organizational and regulatory policies.

The role of the various levels of management is dependent upon the size of the organization, and the number of departments and employees of the organization. In smaller institutions, the vice-president level may be involved in writing protocols on an individual department basis. In larger hospitals, these duties may fall to department managers and supervisors.

At the top of the administrative ledger is the chief executive officer. Like a ship's captain, this individual is responsible for the overall direction and operation of the organization. However, like our ship's captain, this one person can not be every where, at all times; nor can they know every thing about the business, or the industry trends. It would be nearly impossible for a CEO, to have every available piece of information regarding the operations of the company, personnel issues, and how other firms are directing changes to become more efficient. These include disciplines such as finance, nursing, information technology, physician's knowledge and so on. This creates a need for individual to fill the role of vice presidents, department managers, and supervisors of the various sections.

This level of specialization is responsible for collecting information from within the organization and measuring performance. This information is measured within the department and the firm, and also against other organization of similar services and size.

These persons are required have educational experience within their field of expertise, and apply this information to generate the best outcomes. They also compare the performance of their given departments to industry norms. Most of time, they are responsible to collect this data and report to the chief executive officer.

Ideally, the CEO coordinates with the vice-presidents and they chart the best courses of action, uses of resources, and attempt to maximize organizational performance, productivity and customer service.[2]

Given the changing landscape of reimbursement policy, monitoring financial performance plays an ever increasing role in business decisions. The administrative team must work together to determine the best use of these funds to maximize performance. Or, as one CEO said, "if the company has no margin, there is no mission". That is to say, if the company is not making a profit, it will soon be out of business.

Further, with the considerable scope of their duties, vice presidents have department managers to oversee the operations of the various departmental sections. This layer of the chain of command frequently has the responsibility for writing the policies that direct the processes and functions of the individual departments. They also direct technical supervisors, and create an environment that conforms to the mission, vision and values of the company. In addition to the firm's directives, they must also comply with federal, state and local regulations. Once written, these policies are reviewed by the vice-presidents and CEO in order to monitor compliance with these directives.

In the majority of companies the influence of personnel decisions and discipline occurs at the next level of the administration, the supervisors. This occurs because these administrators have direct and daily interactions with the front line personnel.[3]

---

2 Bolster C., Herrere, J. The New Health Care CEO. (May 2010) From Hospitals and Health Networks. (Online). May 31, 2012http://www.hhnmag.com/hhnmag_app/jsp/articledisplay.jsp?dcrpath=HHNMAG/Article/data/05MAY2010/100517HHN_Weekly_Bolster&domain=HHNMAG

3 Washington State Hospital Association: Hospital Administration and Management. (2012). (Online). From (May 31, 2012) http://www.wsha.org/

In many cases, the responsibilities of the supervisor include input, with the department manager, to develop policies and procedures, for their particular institutions. These directives should be written to meet industry and regulatory standards, but must also meet the needs of the physicians and customers of the organization. Again, depending on the size of the company, this role may occur at higher or lower levels of the chain of command, depending upon the size of the company.[4]

The reason that many policies are written at this level is due to the varying skills needed and techniques that are performed at the department, such as the laboratory or radiology. As an example let us review echocardiography, which is form of ultrasound examination. It differs from general ultrasound due to the dynamic nature of the cardiac structure, the hemodynamics of the blood flow through the heart and the design of the equipment. Thus, while many of the principles of general sonography apply, the nature of the procedure requires different skill sets and knowledge. In light of the sub-specialty, the echocardiogram department is a member of the cardiology section, while ultrasound is a member of the radiology department.

Furthermore, while there are industry standards for the performance of a routine echocardiogram, the information may vary depending on the specialty of the institution, such as a pediatric clinic, physician specialty and the indication for the examination.

Physicians

The primary role of physicians is to promote the health of their patients. This includes patient interviews, designing treatment plans, medication orders and recommendation of for laboratory testing.

Physicians have the primary responsibility for making an accurate diagnosis; thorough discussions with the patients about their symptoms and the chief complaint; with nurses who have

files/62/Gov_Bd_Manual_HOSPMANAGEMENT.DOC
4 Umiker's Management Skills for Health Care Supervisor. Charles R. McConnell. Jones and Bartlett. Ontario, New York. 2010. pp.83-89.

recorded vital signs and comments made by the patient regarding their past and current health, and current medications; and the technicians that perform the necessary laboratory examinations required to make the diagnosis.

In addition to these activities, the doctor has a responsibility to ensure that the care plan is medically appropriate and, meets expected risk/reward ratios.[5]

The actions and recommendations of the physician are judged by their customers, the patient. This judgment includes whether the patient feels that the recommended treatment plan is effective, that the outcome meets their expectations, and if the care delivery team provided outstanding customer service. In many cases the payer of the services, most commonly a medical insurance provider, also judges the services for appropriateness, accurate billing information and cost effectiveness of the resulting services, and recommendations.[6]

All of these factors are weighed by the patient, and their families, as they create their perception of the health care provider and the services rendered by the physician. In addition, their conclusions will play a key role in whether the client refers their family and friends to the clinic.

While physicians often do not have direct authority over hospital employees, their attitudes and behaviors have an impact on how "approachable" physician is to the nurses and technical staff with whom they interact.

Non-managers
The primary role of nurses, technicians and support staff is to perform the basic functions of the institution, perform the various activities recommended by the physician, and to follow the organizational policies and procedures, as determined by the administration.

---

5 American Academy of Family Physicians: Primary Care. (2012). (Online) June 2, 2012. http://www.aafp.org/online/en/home/policy/policies/p/primarycare.html

6http://www.hhnmag.com/hhnmag_app/jsp/articledisplay.jsp?dcrpath=HHNMAG/Article/data/03MAR2007/070313HHN_Online_Wittrup&domain=HHNMAG

For hospital in-patients, these "front-line" individuals have more contact, and spend more time with, the patient than either the physician or the administrator.

Most commonly, they are the first persons to meet the customer. This event may occur at the front desk at check-in, or over the phone when scheduling appointments. This creates a first impression and creates an expectation, on the part of the customer, of the attitudes and behaviors of the remaining individuals that will have contact with the patient.

They are also the last contact before the patient physically leaves the hospital. This encounter often provides the last memory of the health care visit and carries great importance in the final perception of the organization.[7]

As an example, during the performance of an echocardiogram, the patient spends thirty minutes to an hour with the sonographer performing the examination. During this time, the care provider has numerous opportunities to create a positive experience for the client. Is the technician friendly, confident and clear in their communications? Do they explain the procedure to the person being examined? Each of these is judged by the patient, and plays a vital role in the perception of the customer service provided by the technician and the organization.

During the inpatient health care visit, the nurse often has the largest role in patient interactions. This is due to the inordinate amount of time, and the responsibilities, of this care provider.

The responsibility of the nurse includes patient comfort, distribution of medications, documenting vital signs, noting comments and complaints, providing explanations of the events that will occur, and addressing the patient's concerns. Nurses are frequently available to the patient on a twenty-four basis, and this creates a bond between the client and the nurse provider. In addition, they often serve as an intermediary with the physicians, and technicians involved with the patient's care.

---

7 http://alliedhealthcouncilslu.org/responsibilities-of-an-allied-health-professional

As a result of the time element, and the services provided, these personnel play a large role in creating an atmosphere of customer service and satisfaction.

In the next chapter we will begin a discussion on the effects of poor communication between the three "legs" of our table affect the work environment and customer service.

CHAPTER 3

THE ROLES OF MIDDLE MANAGERS ON THE WORK ENVIRONMENT

In an article by Leigh Rivenbark, he presents the idea that 90 % of employees leave companies because of their manager, and that 90 % of managers think that the employee leaves because of salary issues.[8]

In some cases the relationship between the manager and the employee is like a long term effect of 'paper cuts'. Paper cuts sting, and, at first, this sensation passes quickly. A few more paper cuts and it stings a little longer. Over a period of a few weeks, months

---

8 The 7 Hidden Reasons Employees Leave: How to Recognize the Subtle Signs and Act Before It's Too Late. Leigh Branham.
AMACOM. New York, N.Y. 2005.

and years the paper cuts add up. They no longer become minor annoyances.

Let us look at one situation that is like those paper cuts. An employee starts a new job and is excited about the new responsibilities, meeting new people, and making a difference in the work environment.

At some point the new supervisor finds fault with some little thing that the individual has done. As an example, there is a coffee maker in thee department break room with coffee available for every employee. You know that there is an unspoken rule that who ever drinks the last of the coffee makes a new pot. Let's say you drink the last of coffee, and you decide not to make more. Perhaps you feel that you are too busy, or that you drink coffee only occasionally, so you should not be held responsible. Your supervisor tells you about the team's expectation that you make more. They tell you that everyone participates in this activity, and that you should do the same. You thank the supervisor for the information and the issue is soon forgotten.

Two weeks go by, and again you take the last cup of coffee on the way to meeting a client. You are in a rush, or that someone else will 'take care of it'. You get another visit form your boss, this time with a little firmer tone. You explain to the boss about your appointment, and that it won't happen again. This is the first paper cut, it is annoying, but you both move on.

Another week and a half, another incident occurs with the coffee. You get half a cup of coffee, leaving just enough in the bottom that you can leave it for the next person. Your boss walks in and sees you leave with the half empty cup. The manager asks why you didn't refresh the coffee, and you say you didn't finish it. You explain that you were busy, but that you just didn't have time. This seems to satisfy the supervisor without further discussion and both leave a little frustrated. Yet somewhere in the back of your mind, you know you have 'gotten away with it' without serious consequence. But, in your manager's mind, this is another paper cut paper and they start to add up.

After a period of time this occurs on a weekly basis. The paper cuts are more frequent; they stop stinging, and begin to really hurt. While not making the coffee is not a company policy, it is an unwritten expectation in the department. So, you feel that while preparing the coffee is expected, it is not a written policy, and the supervisor has no basis for a formal reprimand. While may feel some remorse, you know that you can get away it.

Since the supervisor has formal means of disciplining you, the only recourse to available to them is to scrutinize your work, find fault in every little thing that you do, assign you tasks that you do not like, review your attendance and sick days, and starts to delay, or even deny, your vacation requests. This is one way that they get even with your lack of cooperation.

Moving forward, the relationship between you and your supervisor decays further, and you become more frustrated with one another. Think of how this affects the two employees, the co-workers and customers.

Since you, the employee, feel singled out by the supervisor, you start to spend more time looking over your shoulder. You spend more time worrying about the next time that the manager will find fault than concentrating on your work. As a result, you are constantly distracted, which affects your ability to accurately and efficiently perform your responsibilities. This reduces the quality and efficiency of the performance of your duties. Because of this distraction, you start to make mistakes. Finally, you lose your desire to go to work, be at work, and to be in the work environment.

You make every effort to avoid your manager, even to the point of making an error rather than ask a question of your superior.

This attitude becomes apparent to your co-workers and your customers. You feel a need to frequently share your complaints with your peers, often in an effort to get them on 'your side'. At this point, your co-workers will not want to get in the middle between you and the supervisor. And your clients will not want to work with an individual that does not give them the undivided attention that they feel they deserve.

The supervisor feels that you are disrespectful, untrustworthy and dismissive of authority. As time passes, the resentment builds, and affects the leader's relationships with the other employees. The morale and performance of the department declines, and customers will find other companies for their needs.

In the situation described above, it is easy to look from the outside and see how this relationship failed.

While this is a simple example, this same scenario plays out in work environments every day. Employees grow frustrated with their manager; and the manager grows frustrated with the employee. And, their, and the organization, performance suffers until the employee finds a new job or is forced out of the company.

Either of these results affects the department, and the organization, in several different ways.

There is decreased financial performance. First, there is the loss of trained personnel. Think of the time and energy that has been devoted to train the individual how to perform the tasks and responsibilities of their position. This includes the employee's time in orientation, the time of the person that performed the training, and the materials that were used or lost in the learning activities.

Next, there is the time and energy lost in recruiting to replace the lost employee, including the human resources to place ads, perform interviews and identify a final candidate. Once a permanent employee is hired, the costs associated with training are incurred once again. And depending on the skill levels of the previous employee and the new hire, the costs associated with training may be the cost of training may be higher than the lost employee.

In addition to the cost of replacing a trained employee, many of your customers have forged a relationship with the former team member. Depending on the nature of job, this may have a significant impact on how the client views the 'changed' environment and whether they would continue their relationship with the company.

Finally, the treatment of the employee may impact how the co-workers view the supervisor, and possibly the organization. Did they feel that the administrator was vindictive, and look for an opportunity to leave? Or did they feel that departed personnel behaved inappropriately. In the former instance, they may have poor morale, and not perform up to their expected standard. In the latter, they may be happy that the offending employee has left the department and have a more positive energy to the work environment.

In addition to the financial penalties, there is a longer lasting effect on the reputation of the department.

The remaining employees have to recover from the long standing feud.

An initial effect of the loss of an employee is that the co-workers have to absorb the responsibilities of the departed member. These additionally duties may be a distraction from their own daily activities, or become so burdensome that they may detract from their normal activities. In addition, the relationship between the supervisor and the employees has also been damaged. In many cases, the contentious relationship has built mistrust between the team members, and has affected how the co-workers communicate with one another and the supervisor.

To fully recover, these issues must be addressed over a long period of time.

In addition to employee relations, the organization must rebuild its damaged reputation with its customers.

For clients that have had a relationship with the malcontented employee may be hesitant to deal with the company. In addition these patrons often share their experiences with family and friends, which negatively impacts referral patterns.

All of this occurs because one employee did not feel the need to make coffee.

This is a single, and simple, example of how the relationship between employees can affect the bottom line of a company. There are other numerous and, often, more complex, issues that arise in every day situations that may have dire effects on the organization and people's lives.

How is this reflected in the three legs of our table?

At the top of the corporate ladder is the administration. This starts with the chief executive officer and continues down to the level of the supervisors. At the top levels of the chain of command are the individuals with business educations and backgrounds. They often have a minimum of Master's degrees, often in business and accounting. Many of these individuals have no clinical experience, and, thus, have little, or no, understanding of the clinical processes over which they preside.

The second "leg" of the table, is comprised of the employees who are the nurses, technicians and support staff that perform the daily operations. These persons are specially trained with in their clinical field, and often lack business education and skills. These individuals are highly trained professionals that have little or no business education.

At some point in the chain of command the business administrator presides directly over an individual with a clinical background. This may occur at any level in the corporate health care ladder. This may occur at the vice-president-department manager or manager-supervisor level.

In many of these instances, the manager or supervisor has been selected for promotion based on one of two criteria. The first is technical excellence. This may the better choice, as this person will serve as a role model, teacher and assists in the writing and implementation of department policy. The second criterion is longevity of the individual within the organization or profession. The technician has worked in the department long enough and has knowledge of the department and its culture and provides a high level of value to the organization.[9]

In either case, this individual has limited experience in the business and management side of the position. Many hospitals provide short courses on how to perform measures of productivity, budget and scheduling to allow the individual to function in their new role.[10]

---

9 Umiker's Management Skills for Health Care Supervisor. Charles R. McConnell. Jones and Bartlett. Ontario, New York. 2010. pp.3-4.
10 Eichenberg, R., Lombardo, M. Twenty-two ways to Develop Leadership in Staff Managers. Part 1 of 4. GovLeaders.org. (1990). http://govleaders. org/22ways.htm.

This creates a communication gap. This gap is the result of the differing roles and background of each administrator at the different levels.

In addition to the administration-employee relationship, there is a third member, the physicians. Physicians have a separate, but equally important, role in the field of health care. While many doctors have their own practices, they utilize the services provided by hospitals and various clinics. As a result, physicians are dependent upon the technicians, nurses and other service personnel to perform the activities necessary to provide care and office support. Technical personnel perform the tests that ordered, nurses provide clinical care, and support staff schedule appointments, contact pharmacies, etc.

Well executed communication between the doctor and the employees ensure that the requests of the physician are clear and concise. This information is the basis for follow-up appointments, scheduling examinations and billing purposes. Similarly, an environment must also exist that the technicians a have the ability to approach the care provider to clear up any questions or unresolved issues regarding the follow-up care for the patient.

With regard to technical dependent examinations such as an echocardiogram, it is important that the physician reading examination and the echocardiographer clearly understand what information must be recorded. Various disease states have different findings and may require that additional views and information be obtained. Thus it is important that the physician and the echocardiographer both clearly understand what information is necessary for a complete and accurate study.

Benefits of this type of relationship is that it eliminates the need to repeat studies; better examinations are performed, leading to better care for the patient; and building trust between the technician and the physician.

The next chapter discusses how the importance of corporate culture, and its influences the work environment and the relationships between the members of the three supports of our customer service table.

CHAPTER 4

CORPORATE CULTURE AND ORGANIZATIONAL PERFORMANCE

Every organization has unique sets of interactions and behaviors between administration and employees. And, in health care, there is a third set of individuals that interact with these tow groups, the physician. The pattern of the interactions between these two, or three, groups are referred to as the 'corporate culture'.

Wikipedia defines corporate culture as "the attitudes, experiences, beliefs and values of an organization".[11] These traits permeate through every organization and influence the attitudes and

---

11 Culture- Definition and More from the Free Miriam- Webster Dictionary. (July 7, 2012). Definition of culture. (Online). July 7, 2012. http://www. merriam-webster.com/dictionary/culture.

actions of every level of the chain of command. In addition to an overall corporate culture, there are departmental patterns of behavior that affect the smaller portions of the firm.

The corporate culture defines the perception of each employee's attitude toward the company, managers, and co-workers. Corporate culture may be perceived positively or negatively, and the resulting behaviors affect the employee's overall performance.

The ideal situation is to create an environment in which every member of the organization feel appreciated and respected. One of the keys creating this type of environment is communication that is two-way, open and honest. This type of activity creates an environment in which members have mutual trust and respect for their peers.[12]

Another critical component of the corporate culture occurs when policies are enforced in a fair and balanced manner. The perception that some employees are treated differently results in the perception some employees are a manager's favorite, or that the members of the administration "play politics". Employees that feel this way believe that the manager can not be trusted or that employees should try to get on their "good side". Either one of these situations erodes employee morale and affects the performance of the individuals under their command.[13]

The ideal situation occurs when the corporate culture reflects the company's mission, vision and values. These characteristics, as set forth, should be reflected in every relationship inside and outside of the organization. This behavior should be apparent in every interaction between administrators, employees and physicians.

The mission, vision and values are typically created by the board of directors and the senior administration, and should identify the company's reason for existence, goals, vales and behavioral traits that will guide its employees in achieving these ambitions.[14]

---

12 Unversia Knowledge @ Wharton. (2010, May 19.) Virtuous cycle; how managers can take the lead in building trust at work. (Online) May 13, 2011. http://www.wharton.universia.net/index.cfm?fa=viewArticle&id=1892&language=english

13 Umiker's Management Skills for Health Care Supervisor. Charles R. McConnell. Jones and Bartlett. Ontario, New York. 2010. pp. 271-280.

14 Ibid. pp.29-31.

As these ideals are the creation of the senior management, they are also the responsibility of the top managers to create the environment in which these goals are realized. In addition to enforcement, these individuals should embrace and display these attitudes in their daily behaviors and interactions.

At the top of the organizational chart is the chief executive officer, who bears the ultimate responsibility for ensuring that these ideals are implemented. The CEO should serve as a role model, and plays a large role in creating an environment that supports these lofty expectations.

Most companies adopt the values of communication, honest, trust and respect. It is then incumbent upon the administrative personnel, starting with the CEO, to model these model these behaviors to the next level of the corporate ladder. Organizations that embrace and display these characteristics tend to have employees that display increased loyalty and productivity. Employees that work in this type of environment feel valued by the company and take ownership in their performance, the firm's products and services, and provide the best outcomes for the company and its customers.

As the top executive, it is incumbent upon the chief executive officer to behave in a manner consistent with the mission, vision and values. This individual must display these traits when interacting with the company's vice-presidents. In most instances, humans act and react in the same manner which they are treated by their immediate administrator.[15][16]

In light of this behavioral characteristic, it is important that every administrator, from the CEO down, displays these same attitudes to their peers. Thus, supervisors behave in a manner

---

15 Unversia Knowledge @ Wharton. (2010, May 19.) Virtuous cycle; how managers can take the lead in building trust at work. (Online) May 13, 2011. http://www.wharton.universia.net/index.cfm?fa=viewArticle&id=1892&language=english

16 Bolster C., Herrere, J. The New Health Care CEO. (May 2010) From Hospitals and Health Networks. (Online). May 31, 2012. http://www.hhnmag.com/hhnmag_app/jsp/articledisplay.jsp?dcrpath=HHNMAG/Article/data/05MAY2010/100517HHN_Weekly_Bolster&domain=HHNMAG

similar to the managers, the manager to the vice-president, and the vice-presidents to the CEO. Similarly, the nurses, technicians and support personnel will embody these behaviors in their interactions with customers.

When this type of behavior is embraced, and modeled, throughout the organization, the morale of administrators and employees tend to be a high level. This results in high levels of communication, respect and productivity. Employees take ownership of their own performance, and the overall performance of the company.

Conversely, in organizations that fail to embrace these characteristics, the attitudes and behaviors of the employees erode over a period of time, with a resulting decrease in morale, performance and productivity. Fail to adhere to the mission, vision and values can occur at any level in the organizational chart, and serves to affect the attitudes of the persons under their direction.[17] [18] [19]

Keeping in mind that administrators mimic the behavior of their superior, when deficiencies arise, it is important to look for the 'lowest common denominator'. That is to identify where the break down of the ideal characteristics or behaviors occurs. At this point it is necessary to identify the individual or protocol that is responsible for the poor performance.

As an example, there was an instance in which an employee asked their supervisor for vacation time that coincided with her mother's birthday. The request was made eleven months before the requested time off. The supervisor did not respond when the initial request was made. As the desired dates drew closer, a

---

17 Knowledge@Wharton (2006, November 15). More than job demands or personality, lack of organizational respect fuels employee burnout. (Online) May 13, 2011.

18 Northwestern University (n.d.) Forum for People Performance and Measurement; Executive Summary: Linking organizational characteristics to employee attitudes and behaviors: a look at the downstream effects on market response & financial performance. (Online) May 14, 2011.
http://www.incentivecentral.org/pdf/employee_engagement_study.pdf

19 Umiker's Management Skills for Health Care Supervisor. Charles R. McConnell. Jones and Bartlett. Ontario, New York. 2010. pp. 38.

decision was delayed, with the explanation that the department was short staffed, and that necessitated a delay in approval. In the meantime, other vacations by co-workers were granted.

Two weeks before the employee's requested time off, the supervisor was approached about the issue once again. The supervisor again refused the request. On week later the employee quit.

There are several issues that arise in the example.

First, the date of the original request allowed the supervisor to adequately recruit the resources that were necessary to cover the vacated shifts. The supervisor failed to plan for a valuable employee, and this conveys the message that the employee, and their efforts, was not valued by the supervisor.

Second, other employees were granted vacation requests. This suggests that the supervisor was "playing favorites". Again, this acts as a signal that the supervisor does not respect or value the employee.

With respect to this example, the employee felt that they were not respected by their supervisor, and were frustrated that they were unable to identify a solution that would meet her needs and the needs of the organization. In a discussion with this employee, she felt that other co-workers had a similar frustration, and that efforts to remedy the situation with human resources and upper administration fell on deaf ears.[20]

In an article by Barsdale and Ramarajan, they discuss the idea that employee burn out is sometimes a result of the organizational culture. The employee in this instance felt frustrated, and ultimately, led to the employee feeling "burned out" by the behaviors the employee's superiors.[21]

In a department that already faces staffing difficulties, these attitudes will affect the ability of the department to maintain adequate personnel levels. As a result, the department can not

---

20 The 7 Hidden Reasons Employees Leave: How to Recognize the Subtle Signs and Act Before It's Too Late. Leigh Branham. AMACOM. New York, N.Y. 2005.

21 Knowledge@Wharton (2006, November 15) More than job demands or personality, lack of organizational respect fuels employee burnout. (Online) May 13, 2011.
http://knowledge.wharton.upenn.edu/article.cfm?articleid=1600

adequately meet its responsibilities; employee morale plummets, and customers are affected by decreased productivity and the evident attitudes of the employees.

In looking at other situations of poor department culture, it may be necessary to re-evaluate the policies and personnel of the offending service. Stressors that may arise include adequate staffing levels, poorly designed organizational directives, or policies that directly affect the work environment or the personnel.[22]

As an example, some echocardiography departments require that a technician's worksheet be completed immediately after the performance of an echocardiogram. While this should be a standard, on occasion, it may delay the technician from attending to another patient, or procedure, which may disrupt the flow of the department, its nurses and physicians. This situation may be necessary if a patient delayed from echo laboratory, and the technician needs to "catch up' to their schedule. In this instance, it may be necessary to perform two, possibly three, examinations before completing the necessary paperwork to best facilitate the department schedule.

Conversely, the echocardiography technician *should* complete their worksheets in a timely manner, so that the interpreting physician may complete their reports in a timely manner.

It would be important to perform a thorough review of this policy and ensure that the policy have some flexibility. Sometimes the easiest answer, in this case the worksheet being completed after every exam, does not always provide the best service or overall productivity.

Despite the idea that employees display the same behaviors and attitudes as their superior, every employee has their own unique personality, values and beliefs. These differing character traits affect how they perceive their work environment, performance levels, and how they interact with other persons. As a result, while the characteristics modeled by the CEO, or other administrators, influence the next level of the chain of command, this is not an absolute.

---

22 Umiker's Management Skills for Health Care Supervisor. Charles R. McConnell. Jones and Bartlett. Ontario, New York. 2010. pp. 83-87.

In the end, each individual responds to the corporate culture, their superiors, and the performance of the work differently. These individual sets of values and beliefs should be respected, but the employee's performance and productivity should meet department expectations.

In addition their administrators, health care workers are also influenced by attitudes and behaviors of the physicians with whom they interact. As such, physicians be should also held accountable to the values of the organization. Yet, most physicians are, independent contractors with the health care institutions that they serve. As discussed previously, they often have their own practices and make financial and business decisions that meet their needs. This creates a situation where it is vitally important that the hospital administration and the doctor have clearly defined common goals to minimize frustrations between the parties.

Given the role of the physician, acting as a director of the patient care, they have a responsibility to ensure that the proper levels of care are provided, and that testing procedures are conducted in a timely and efficient manner. As a result, they must a have a level of authority over service personnel to ensure that their directives are performed and reported in an accurate and timely fashion.[23]

Thus, the behaviors and attitudes of the physician toward employees contribute to the morale and performance of the nurses, technicians and support staff.

In looking at echocardiography for an example, a patient with dynamic obstruction of the left ventricular outflow tract, such as hypertrophic obstructive cardiomyopathy, presents a technical challenge. Properly documenting the degree of disease may be complicated by the presence of calcific disease of the aortic valve.[24]

---

23 http://heart.bmj.com/content/82/suppl_3/III8.full

http://www.hhnmag.com/hhnmag_app/jsp/articledisplay.jsp?dcrpath=HHNMAG/Article/data/03MAR2007/070313HHN_Online_Wittrup&domain=HHNMAG
24

Hypertrophic obstructive cardiomyopathy, or HOCM, is defined by a thickening of the interventricular septum which creates a narrow region of blood flow exiting the left ventricle. This creates an abnormal motion of the mitral valve into the opening that decreases the amount of blood flow out of the left ventricle. As the outflow tract area decreases, the velocity of flow through this area increases. In addition, there are several maneuvers that increase the severity of the obstruction.

While performing the echocardiogram, the sonongrapher must understand the condition, as well as have an understanding of how to best document the cardiac abnormality. This assists the physician in making a proper diagnosis and determines if treatment protocols are indicated. A clear understanding of the information necessary to aid the physician reduces the need to repeat the examination.

From this example, it is apparent that health care workers are influenced by attitudes and behaviors of the physicians, as well as their administrators. As such, physicians be should also held accountable to the values of the organization. Yet, most physicians are, independent contractors with the health care institutions that they serve. They often have their own practices and have are required make financial and business decisions that meet their needs. This creates a situation where it is vitally important that the hospital administration and the doctor have clearly defined common goals to minimize frustrations between the parties.

Given the role of the physician, serving as the director of the patient's care, they have a responsibility to ensure that the proper levels of care are provided, and that testing procedures are conducted in a timely and efficient manner. As a result, they must a have a level of authority over service personnel to ensure that their directives are performed and reported in an accurate and timely fashion.[25]

As a result, the behaviors and attitudes of the physician toward employees contribute to the morale and performance of the nurses, technicians and support staff.

25http://www.hhnmag.com/hhnmag_app/jsp/articledisplay. jsp?dcrpath=HHNMAG/Article/data/03MAR2007/070313HHN_Online_ Wittrup&domain=HHNMAG

Finally, organizations sometimes adopt buzz words, catch phrases and motivational programs in order to build employee morale. While phrases like 'you can choose your own attitude', and 'hard work is own reward' may sounds good, they only work on individuals that already have a good attitude or work hard.

The limitation of these efforts is that, in many cases, that administration has created a poor corporate culture. There is a low level of communication and minimal amount of respect. Thus, despite how badly the employees feel they have been treated, the organization feels that the employee should have a good attitude.

One of the prevailing ideas is that they "should be happy that they have a job". Yet there are numerous reports, as discussed later, that salary and bonuses serve as poor motivational tools.

The most effect types of motivation occur when leaders serve as good role models, create effective communication, and give positive recognition of performance and behaviors. This occurs because employees frequently imitate the characteristics and behaviors of their supervisor and managers.[26]

Supervisors that create this kind positive, learning and communicative environment provide a very strong and powerful leadership model. The individuals that work for them feel appreciated and are motivated by this activity, perform at a higher level, and provide better customer support.

A Gallup poll study reports that organizations that have employees that are more engaged in the company are happier, more productive and responsive to change. The result was increased customer satisfaction and retention.[27]

Another motivation technique is through monetary compensation. The problem with type of approach is that employees often feel that salary reflects their importance to the company.

---

26 Umiker's Management Skills for Health Care Supervisor. Charles R. McConnell. Jones and Bartlett. Ontario, New York. 2010. pp. 172-177.

27 Gallup Poll. (2010). Employee engagement: what's your engagement ratio? (Brochure.) (Online). May 13, 2011.
http://www.google.com/search?sourceid=navclient&aq=0&oq=employee+engagement+what%27s+&ie=UTF-8&rlz=1T4HPIB_enUS313US313&q=employee+engagement+what%27s+your+engagement+ratio

Thus they feel that the company "owes" them the salary figure which they are receiving. As a result of this attitude, pay raises and bonuses are become routine expectation, and serve to create only a limited influence on the morale and performance. In addition, when these extra pay raises and bonuses are no longer given, there is a feeling of resentment.[28]

As a result, pay increases and bonuses should never be used as motivational tools, but should reflect the skills and expectations of the individual and the services that they provide.[29]

Administrators that embrace an environment of learning, respect and support show better long term efforts in creating improved employee morale and performance. Employee feel that the manager, and by extension the organization, care about the employee. There becomes a symbiotic atmosphere of respect and loyalty.

Organizations that embrace a culture of communication, learning, and sharing, encourage better team work between its members, and better performance from the employees. These behaviors and attitudes also engender feelings of respect and confidence, which become evident in their attitude, and their work. Often customers sense these traits and attitudes, and have increased confidence and trust with the individual that is working with them. Thus, they are more likely to create a bond with this person, and report positive experience to the care being given or to the services being provided.

---

28 Gallup Poll. (2010). Employee engagement: what's your engagement ratio? (Brochure.) (Online). May 13, 2011.
http://www.google.com/search?sourceid=navclient&aq=0&oq=employee+engagement+what%27s+&ie=UTF-8&rlz=1T4HPIB_enUS313US313&q=employee+engagement+what%27s+your+engagement+ratio
29 Umiker's Management Skills for Health Care Supervisor. Charles R. McConnell. Jones and Bartlett. Ontario, New York. 2010. pp. 212-213.

CHAPTER 5

CUSTOMER SERVICE AND CUSTOMER SATISFACTION

Outstanding customer service is never an accident. Instead it is a dedication to strategies and behaviors that arise from dedicated employees from every level of the organizational ladder.

In health care, the best customer service occurs when employees from all three legs of our table work in harmony to achieve the best outcomes. Some of the characteristics of this ideal is timely and effective communication, information sharing, caring and respect. Given the level of trust that patients place in the hands of the care provider, they have increased levels of perception and sensitivity to the attitudes and behaviors of the health care professionals.[30]

This heightened awareness is made through their observations of the environment and personnel of the health care clinic. They judge the appearance and cleanliness of the clinic and the employees, as well as the behaviors and attitudes of the providers, including perceptions of attentiveness, confidence, skill and knowledge levels.[31]

In the performance of a routine office visit, many patients have an expectation of service and performance on the part of the health care professionals. In most instances they have had appointments at the same clinic, and expect a similar experience as the visit unfolds.

When the patient is the referred for further examinations, they may not be familiar with the processes and procedures that may be prescribed. As a result, the client may experiences an elevated level of apprehension with the approaching examination.

In this event, customer service on the part of the health care provider is of paramount importance. The patient may not have been informed what the test entails, how it is performed, or what they experience may during the performance of the examination. Examples of questions on the part of the patient may include 'will it hurt' or 'does it involve a shot or needles'. It is also important for the patient to understand what sensations the patient may experience. For instance, during an angiogram the contrast agent may cause a flushing sensation. In this case, it would be important for the health care provider to explain the odd feeling, in an effort to allow the patient to know that this is a normal reaction. Other questions that arise include "how long before I get the results", and "who gives me the final report?"

In addition to judging the responses to their questions, the patient will judge the sonographer by their perception of the skill level of the individual performing the examination. This

---

30 Bierig, M., Ehler, D., et.al. Minimum Standards for the Cardiac Songrapher: A Position Paper. (2012). (Online). (May 30, 2012). From http://www.asefiles. org/sonographerminimumstandards.pdf

31 Do Patients Equate Cleanliness with Quality. (Sep 2002). From http://www.gallup.com/poll/6784/Patients-Equate-Cleanliness-Quality.aspx

judgment is based on visual clues, such as the technician's confidence level, the ability to acquire clear images, and responses to verbal questioning, such as an inquiry into their training and experience.

In the event of the patient having their first echocardiogram, they are unaware of how the procedure is performed; if it requires needles or injections; is the procedure painful; what information is obtained; and how and when will they get the results.

Because of all these unknowns the sonographer plays a critical role in providing the answers and creating a safe environment. Relaying a brief introduction to the procedure, that it uses sound waves to image the heart, and that is non-invasive will relieve some of the patient's initial anxiety.

Before the start of the length of the procedure, the echocardiographer may suggest a visit to the restroom. As these examinations routinely take 30 minutes to an hour to perform, this may alleviate patient discomfort during the procedure, and avoid interruption of the test.

Sonograms, including echocardiograms, involve the use of a coupling agent, or gel, which at room temperature, is feels cold when it contacts the skin. The patient should be warned of this phenomenon, so that they can prepare themselves for the chilling sensation. Explaining to the patient that the coupling agent is necessary for the performance of the procedure is explained to allow the individual prepare for the gel.

Additionally, the echocardiographer may educate the patient about the cardiac anatomy and blood flow by explaining the structures on the screen and the role of each structure. This would include identification and function of each the chambers and valves. Using expressions such as the left ventricle pumps the blood to the body, helps to create a better experience for the patient.

Echocardiograms are routinely performed with the patient lying on their left side. Using this type of position aids in the demonstration of the cardiac structures, and this information should be shared with the patient.

In addition, the sonographer may explain how breathing techniques will assist the professional in obtaining the information necessary for proper interpretation. It may be explained that the ultrasonic beam does not record images that are blocked by the lungs and the ribs. As a result, there are limited windows that allow imaging, and that these may be improved by held inspiration and expiration. By using held inspiration, or expiration, obstruction resulting from the lungs and ribs is reduced.

Echocardiography, in most circumstances, is performed with patients that are conscious and alert. During the performance of the echocardiogram the monitor may be positioned in a location that may be viewed by the patient. Often patients will express an interest in what is being displayed on the screen. While industry and local standards preclude the sonographer from providing diagnostic information, in they can identify the cardiac structures and explain what the Doppler signals represent. As an example, showing the left ventricle and explaining that it is the chamber which pumps the blood to the body. Or that the color Doppler shows the blood flow within the heart, with red being flow into heart and blue out of the heart, as a general rule.

It should be understood, and explained to the patient, that the sonographer may share very limited information, and should never create a situation in which a diagnosis may be inferred.

Because of the patient's curiosity, and the nature of the procedure, sonographers can create an environment in which the patient "participates" in the examination. By explaining how they can participate in obtaining a complete examination, such as proper positioning or breath holding, the patient becomes invested in assisting the technician achieve an optimal study.[32]

Finally, the echocardiographer should routinely explain to the patient that the information obtained will be reviewed by a cardiologist that will dictate a final report. As each institution has differing methods of disseminating this information, the sonographer may indicate how, and when, the patient will receive the results.[33]

32 Bierig, M., Ehler, D., et.al. Minimum Standards for the Cardiac Songrapher: A Position Paper. (2012). (Online) From http://www.asefiles.org/sonographerminimumstandards.pdf (May 30, 2012).

33 Bierig, M., Ehler, D., et.al. Minimum Standards for the Cardiac Songrapher: A Position Paper. (2012). (Online) From http://www.asefiles.org/sonographerminimumstandards.pdf (May 30, 2012).

Given the role of the health care professional during the procedure and the responsibility acquiring a diagnostic examination, it becomes apparent that this individual has a great influence on the patient's perception of the customer service that is provided.[34] [35]

In addition to the role that the technician plays in providing direct customer support, this care provider may directly affect patient care. During the performance of an echocardiogram, the technician's interactions may lead to uncovering information vital to the outcome of the patient visit. The knowledge gathered during the discussion may include further signs and symptoms that ma be relayed to the physician to assist in creating an appropriate treatment plan.[36]

Let me relay a personal experience of a patient-echocardiographer-physician encounter in which communication created a best and timely outcome.

During the performance of an echocardiogram at an outreach clinic, a patient related that he experienced chest pains every time he wrestled playfully with his sons. Knowing that one of the signs of coronary artery disease is chest pain related to exertion efforts, the technician made a recommendation that the patient should meet with the cardiologist that was in the same location.

The physician consented to the appointment and conducted an interview. The doctor had similar concerns regarding the chest pain, and recommended further testing to be conducted. After an electrocardiogram was performed, the patient was referred for a cardiac catherization, which displayed significant narrowing of the coronary arteries. As a result of this invasive procedure,

---

34Ehler, D., Carney, D. (Jan. 2001). Guidelines for Cardiac Songrapher Education Recommendations of the American Society of Echocardiography Sonographer Training and Education Committee. (Online) From: http://www.asefiles.org/sonographereducation.pdf

35 See My Heart: Information for Patients on Heart Ultrasound (Echocardiography). (2012). (Online) From http://www.asecho.org/i4a/pages/index.cfm?pageid=3326

36 Bierig, M., Ehler, D., et.al. Minimum Standards for the Cardiac Songrapher: A Position Paper. (2012). (Online). From http://www.asefiles.org/sonographerminimumstandards.pdf (May 30, 2012).

coronary artery bypass graft surgery was performed, and the patient had a successful recovery.

The due diligence of the echocardiographer, and the requisite conversation with the physician enabled a proper diagnosis and course of treatment. Additionally, the patient later expressed his appreciation to the staff members for the level of services that was provided.

As can be reasoned from this example, an open and respectful relationship between physician and technician serves enhance customer service and may positively influence the diagnosis and outcomes of a health care visit.

It should be recognized that while this example is between physician and technician, it must be remembered that these types of interactions and dynamics occur in between physicians, nurses and support personnel.[37] These activities occur on a routine basis each day, and create a positive environment for every member of the organization.

Conversely, a strained relationship between the physician and technician serves to hamper this relationship.

In the example presented above, if the doctor and sonographer have a difficult relationship, this may make the technician reticent to share information with the physician. Coronary artery disease, by echocardiography, is documented by reduced activity of the myocardium. Echocardiograms are routinely performed at rest. As the patient discussed that symptoms only occurred with physical activity, a sonogram performed at rest may not have recorded an abnormality. In this event, the client may have been discharged from the clinic and may later have suffered a heart attack. The collaboration between the health care professionals lead to an accurate assessment of the symptoms and contributed to the proper course of action.

Similar types of situations arise between nurses and other health care providers, the accurate and timely reporting of this information is necessary to obtain the best diagnostic and treatment protocols.

---

37 Ehler, D., Carney, D. (Jan. 2001). Guidelines for Cardiac Songrapher Education Recommendations of the American Society of Echocardiography Sonographer Training and Education Committee. (Online) From: http://www.asefiles.org/sonographereducation.pdf

CHAPTER 6

FAMILIARITY AND THE NEED FOR DIVERSITY IN THE WORK PLACE

According to Sigmund Freud, and others, people are immediately attracted to people that look, think or act like themselves. This trait is seen in the people we choose to have as acquaintances, friends as co-workers. In other words, people are attracted to other individuals, or groups, that have similar ideas and thoughts.[38]

In the corporate world, this creates an almost innate and unspoken bond between co-workers. In this type of environment, feelings of mutual trust and admiration are built easily and

---

38 Sigcarlfred.com. (2005, May 16) People like people like themselves. (Online) May 14, 2011. http://sigcarlfred.blogspot.com/2005/05/people-like-people-like-themselves.html

with little effort. There are numerous advantages of these types of attitudes and behaviors.

First, we believe that those around us will behave in a manner similar to our own, and share many of our own beliefs and values. In many cases, the biggest benefit of this type of work environment is an improvement in morale and performance between team members. In this type of climate, common goals and habits are quickly developed adopted by the co-workers. As an example, in a book club that is dedicated to the writings of a particular author, such as Shakespeare, the members of the group quickly and easily bond and feel a common connection.

In the business environment, this characteristic affects the way individuals feel about their work environment. In addition, this attitude affects how well the worker performs their duties, their productivity and the affects the overall morale of the employee.[39]

In situations where co-workers think and perform in a similar pattern alike, there is a "group think" environment in which expectations of performance and behavior are quickly created. When this occurs, it quickly results in improved interactions with co-workers and customers. Another benefit of this type of environment is that, due to the similar thinking patterns and expectations, employees are allowed more autonomy.

In looking at this situation from a managerial perspective, this behavioral characteristic has a strong influence on personnel decisions. This includes decision making with regard to hiring, promotion and disciplinary activities.

Yet, there are also pitfalls to this type of departmental culture.

If the influence of this 'group think' is prevalent, then employees within this department that display the same characteristics as the majority are given preferred status. When the supervisor adopts this culture, the employees that display the accepted behaviors receive preferential treatment.

---

39 Northwestern University (n.d.) Forum for People Performance and Measurement; Executive Summary: Linking organizational characteristics to employee attitudes and behaviors: a look at the downstream effects on market response & financial performance. (Online) May 14, 2011.http://www. incentivecentral.org/pdf/employee_engagement_study.pdf

This kind of prejudice creates an environment in which everyone thinks the same, and employees most often agree with the manager and change becomes difficult, if not impossible, to employ. In addition, a particular set of behaviors becomes the norm, and non-conforming persons, and behaviors, are met with isolation and harsh disciplinary actions.

While this type of environment is gratifying to the administrator and the conforming employees, it becomes the culture of the affected division. In rare cases, this behavior infiltrates other sections of the company, and potentially becomes pervasive through the entire organization.

When this type of environment is allowed to continue, it may serve as source of frustration for other employees, divisions and, potentially, companies that interact with the offending department or organization.

The greatest pitfall of this behavior is that a single set of behaviors and attitudes become acceptable with in the given group of employees or divisions. This often results in a reduced capacity to accept change, welcome new co-workers, or to identify ways to improve work processes.[40]

The first idea is that familiarity breeds contempt. Freud, and others, asserts that over a period of time other beliefs and characteristics of each individual present themselves. For instance, let us say that an expected behavior is that employees have coffee with the supervisor every morning at 9 AM.

This is a great exercise for team building, and serves to build teamwork and improve team and employee morale.

As an example of the perils of this type of expectation, let us say that a new employee is hired, and that they initially participate in this ritual. Over time, the new hire, who does not like coffee to begin with, starts to choose to drink hot tea. Since there is preparation time to make the beverage, the employee's attendance is delayed from the appointed time.

This new pattern of behavior defies the accepted departmental culture, and, over time, leads to difficult feelings between the

---

40 Zaleznik, A. Managers and leaders: Are they different? Harvard Business Review. Harvard Business Review. 82(1), 74-81.

employees. The new co-worker has violated an unwritten rule of the team. This leads to resentment on the part of the original members of the team, and may cause hard feelings between the co-workers and, potentially, the supervisor.

In this event, teamwork rapidly diminishes, performance is affected and, ultimately, customer service is negatively impacted.

While this may be a simple type of example, this kind behavior creates an environment in which everyone thinks and acts the same. At some point, the accepted behaviors and attitudes create an environment in which even minor change becomes difficult, if not impossible, to employ. In addition, the particular set of characteristics becomes the norm, and non-conforming persons, are met with frustration, and, potentially, disciplinary actions.

Another pitfall of this type of environ anent is that it makes it difficult to accept new team members.

After years of working together, employees learn what behaviors, attitudes and work ethic to expect from their co-workers. Again, there are unwritten rules of accepted behaviors, and the new hire is expected adhere to the former departmental script. If this individual readily fits into the expected role they become almost immediately accepted. If they deviate from the norm, they may be ostracized from their co-workers. The result is team work and performance of the department suffers.

In looking at the future, health care is facing overwhelming challenges and changes.[41] Given the rapid changing conditions that affect health care, this lack of flexibility may handcuff the organization, or just a given department, in the adoption of new practices. Every health care organization must be able to adjust their practices and processes in order to meet these new challenges.

All of the factors that have been discussed may serve to erode the morale of the team members; build distrust; and create an environment of distrust.

When these types of situations arise, it is important that administration intervenes and addresses the malignant attitudes.

---

41 Zaleznik, A. Managers and leaders: Are they different? Harvard Business Review. Harvard Business Review. 82(1), 74-81.

The longer that the destructive attitudes are present, the more that employee morale and customer service is negatively impacted. Thus, it is important that problems be identified and remedied as soon as possible.

The level of activity to resolve these situations is dependent upon the amount of deviation from the norm, and the amount of resentment on the part of the individuals involved in the discrepancy.

For instance, looking at the previous example of the morning coffee incident, the duties of the new employee may arranged differently to allow time to make the tea drinker ample time to prepare for the morning gathering. Another option includes temporarily suspending, or even reducing the frequency of, the morning ritual until the new team member becomes acclimated to their co-workers. Finally, disbanding this behavior may be necessary, while searching for other options that create a common opportunity that satisfies all of the parties involved.

In more difficult circumstances, such as a radical change in the performance of procedure, it may be necessary for the manager to have a hands-on approach to ensure that the new policy is enforced.

While it is important to have a team of persons that enjoy working together, the relationship between the team members should be built upon a base of mutual trust, respect and communication.

It is important to recognize that each member of any team will have different strengths, skills, and knowledge. In the best functioning teams, every individual draws upon others and their specialized abilities. By sharing information, employees improve their skills and knowledge, and this in turn, builds trust and respect.[42]

Echocardiography, specifically, is a technician dependent. The skill and knowledge of the sonographer determine the quality of the images and information that is acquired during the performance of an examination. In an environment of respect

---

42 The 7 Hidden Reasons Employees Leave: How to Recognize the Subtle Signs and Act Before It's Too Late. Leigh Branham. AMACOM. New York, N.Y. 2005.

and learning, technician share their skills, and ask for assistance from other sonographers that have talents that will enhance their study.

The result is a department which the technicians work better with each other, obtains the best information, performs the best examinations and provides the best patient care.

An additional benefit of this type of environment is that processes and procedures are constantly being discusses between the co-workers. This may lead to ideas and suggestions that will improve the quality and efficiency of the task being performed. Adoption of these new processes by the administrator, and physician, if indicated, allows the employees to be involved in the evolution of the department.

This environment may best be achieved under a supervisor that displays the habits and attitudes that are often associated with a leader.

The next chapter starts a discussion of the importance of identifying and developing leaders in the professional organization.

CHAPTER 7

WHY ORGANIZATIONS NEED LEADERS

The characteristics of a good leader are not contained in a box of magic on the chief executive officer's desk. Nor are they limited to the upper echelons of the corporate ladder.

Instead, in most organizations, leaders may be found at every level of any organizational chart. While leadership is usually viewed as the domain of the boards of directors and chief executive officers, this trait is also be evident in the nurses, technicians and support personnel of the every health care institution.[43]

Leaders are individuals that embrace the corporation's vision and values and serve as role models for their fellow employees. They take pride in their work, the department that they work and

---

43 Umiker's Management Skills for Health Care Supervisor. Charles R. McConnell. Jones and Bartlett. Ontario, New York. 2010. pp. 171-182

company that they serve. They are enthusiastic, energetic and consistently go out of their way to assist their co-workers and customers. They act as teachers, students and friends. They work with their team mates to provide high levels of performance, creating new ideas and solutions, and seek to improve each and every day.

These types of individuals earn their respect of peers because of their knowledge, skills, and, quite often, an outgoing personality. Many of these individuals gain strength from outside of themselves, often from successes of their co-workers and peers. These persons perform at the highest levels and, frequently, with only small amounts of reward or recognition. In many cases, these individuals derive their greatest satisfaction when their co-workers and the department achieve higher levels of success and performance.

The importance of a leader can never be understated. These individuals are self-motivated, encourage growth and learning, and create an environment in which team members feel valued and appreciated, perform at a higher level, and often look for the approval of other leaders.

Leaders use verbal and non-verbal methods of communication. They may use discussion to stimulate ideas and actions of peers or to show appreciation of the performance of others. Given their work ethic and level of involvement, they serve as role models for other individuals. In other words, their actions provide a pattern for co-workers to imitate. Since they enjoy creating a dynamic environment, they usually provide unusually high levels of enthusiasm and customer service.[44]

While some individuals may display the characteristics of a leader, it is difficult for some individuals, to develop these skills without a mentor, someone who has established themselves as leader. The role of a mentor is to share the ideas, knowledge and skills that are needed to reach this level.

In others words, leaders create more leaders.

As an example, one nurse-leader kept a candy jar on her desk that was filled with miniature candy bars. This way, her office,

---

44 Ibid.

and the candy were always available to her employees, and they could help themselves when ever they desired.

I think that this action promoted several key ideals.

First, by encouraging employees to enter her office at a time of their own choosing, it reduced the anxiety that many employees have at being in supervisor's office. Most individuals feel that being called into the supervisor's office is like being called to the principal's office at school. It expected that the reason for the visit it discuss an error of judgment or performance. You never expect a good outcome being called into the principal's, or supervisor's, office. Most of us expect some kind of a reprimand of some sort, and prepare to face some kind of consequences.

In the case of my mentor, a visit to her, or the supervisor's office, involved a reward, which created a more positive, and inviting, environment.

Second, it increased the number of contacts with the employees. Most employees, after helping themselves to the treat, would say 'thank you' to the head nurse. It also encouraged the nurses, technicians and support personnel to stay and talk with her on a regular basis. These conversations would be of a relaxed and informal nature, and again served to lower the level of anxiety of visiting with this leader.

Third, the informal nature of the reward created an opportunity for the employee to self-reward themselves. The chocolate could be used by the individual as a positive reinforcement for a task that they felt was above their standard. It also, sometimes, was a way to de-stress after a difficult examination or encounter. This type of self-reward promotes autonomy by allowing the technician to determine when it was appropriate. It also provided self-motivation, because of the ability to self-reward after an above average performance.

In addition to the reward, or treat, it provided an opportunity to share with the supervisor the success that they had achieved, or to discuss the difficult situation in an effort. In the instances of a tough patient or situation, it sometimes necessary to "get it off your chest" with a co-worker, or a leader, just to de-stress, or how the situation may have had a better resolution.

Another type of a reward system is encouraging employees to perform routine, and often mundane, duties. One example involves stocking a supply cabinet that needed to be stocked every nursing shift. After checking, and re-stocking the supplies, a check list was completed, documented that the task was completed. This was a task that could be performed by any of the nurses, with no one individual assigned the responsible of performing this task. And, since no one nurse was assigned the task, the stocking of the closet become haphazard.

In an effort to modify the behaviors of her employees, she would, on random occasions, leave a king size candy bar in a supply cabinet that needed to be stocked. As the candy bar were placed on a "random" basis- different shifts, different days of the week- the head nurse provided a motivation to perform the routine action of stocking the supply cabinet. Also, since the cabinet had to be opened to determine if the treat was there, and the nurse had to document the stocking of the cabinet, necessitating a deliberate effort on the part of a nurse to gain the reward.

The purpose of the king size candy bars was to modify the behavior of the nurses. The larger candy bars are more expensive, and are worth more as a reward. Not only is the motivation effort more expensive for the supervisor, but it also important that the employees maintain the perception that the candy bars become expected every time they perform a certain behavior or task, but that they are positive reinforcement of that activity. In the case of the king size candy bars, a two week time frame, and the idea of rotating them between three shifts, creates a random pattern. This random pattern motivates the nurses to stock the supply cabinet, but does not create the idea that on a given day or time that the gift will be available.

Finally, once the behavior has been modified, the rewards should be discontinued.

Other rewards should be thought of in a similar manner. For instance, a verbal reward such as 'good job, is probably appropriate once a week. This simple gesture, when used, indicates to the individual that you have noticed, and appreciate, their extra efforts.

Written documentation of a behavior, action or performance should match the level of the activity. Many organizations have employee feedback forms. These document, in the employee's file, either a singular outstanding action, or a pattern of ongoing performance above normal expectations. Again, using this type of recognition should be used with a degree of restraint, so that they maintain a feeling of being special. On the other hand, they should not be so difficult to achieve that no employee would ever receive them.

As the reward or recognition associated with a reward increases, the significance of the employee's action should also be increased. For instance, recognition at an organizational level, or the receipt of gift certificates, or cash rewards, should be used to recognize performance levels that are above and beyond a reasonable level of expectation of any employee of the organization. These types of rewards are almost always achieved on once a year basis.

Depending on the nature of the recipient, and the reward, rewards should be given on a personal basis, and often in a private environment. Reward and recognition is personal, most employees gain self-respect from the positive feedback of their manager. It improves the individual's self-confidence, and thy feel that the supervisor cares and respects them as a peer.

Only treats, such as the candy bars, that have minimal significance associated with them should be shared in among other team members. The sharing of a personal recognition with other employees should occur with great caution, as it may be an embarrassment to the individual being recognized. When recognizing an employee for individual accomplishment it should be done on a limited basis, and only with the goal of either educating the other employees of an achievement, and used to motivate other employees to improve their credentials or work performance.

Reward and recognition is personal, and most employees gain self-respect from the positive recognition of their manager. This improves the individual's self-confidence, motivation and job satisfaction. In addition, it tells the employee that the supervisor recognizes their accomplishments.

Almost all employees demonstrate a better response to positive reinforcement than to criticisms. Positive comments elevate self-confidence, makes them feel appreciated, and motivate persons to provide higher levels of performance.[45]

Like praise, negative feedback, and disciplinary actions should always be performed in a private setting, and usually in the supervisor's office. Critical remarks serve diminish the individual's self-image and self-respect. This often results in withdrawal from the social circle of co-workers, feelings of inadequacy, and results in decreased performance and customer service. In addition, these traits are often evident to peers and employees, and serves to reduce the confidence of peers and clients in the employee and disrupt the overall customer service of the department.[46]

When providing negative feedback, it is always important to end the discussion with encouragement and a plan for improvement. In a paper titled "Don't Grade My Paper, Help Me Make an A", the author discusses how he performs performance appraisal at the beginning if the work calendar. The employee and manager set goals, and then meet quarterly to ensure that the goals will be met at year's end.[47]

In addition, the manager is also responsible for the employee meeting the goals, and plays an active role in the success of the employee.

This creates a positive performance evaluation process, while year end evaluations are often provided as the first, and last, employee evaluation on a yearly basis. In this type of situation, the employee is held solely accountable for their performance with little or no feedback during the past 12 month period. Employees often approach these meetings with trepidation due to the lack of input from the superior.

---

45 Umiker's Management Skills for Health Care Supervisor. Charles R. McConnell. Jones and Bartlett. Ontario, New York. 2010. pp. 171-183.

46 Umiker's Management Skills for Health Care Supervisor. Charles R. McConnell. Jones and Bartlett. Ontario, New York. 2010. pp.191-196

47 Blanchard, K., Ridge, G. Helping People Win at Work: Don't Grade My Paper Help Me Make an A. Polvera Publishing. Upper Saddle, River, N.J. 2009.

Sadly, there is a small minority of employees that are difficult to motivate. These individuals frequently find a minimum level performance that will allow them to achieve satisfactory evaluations. In dealing with these types of persons, the effect of positive reinforcement often results in little, if any, motivation. Some of these employees can be motivated through rewards and positive motivation, and with a goal of creating solidly consistent performers.

Leaders learn how their employees respond to these differing stimuli, and then adjust their own behaviors and actions to achieve the best performance from each individual, and the department as a whole.[48]

Finally, leaders do not see obstacles, just opportunities.

Or, in the words of Mother Teresa: "We the willing, led by the unknowing, are doing the impossible for the ungrateful. We have done so much, with so little, for so long, we are now qualified to do anything, with nothing."

---

48 Umiker's Management Skills for Health Care Supervisor. Charles R. McConnell. Jones and Bartlett. Ontario, New York. 2010. pp.191-196

CHAPTER 8

THE NEED TO BUILD LEADERS

Up to this point, we have talked about situations between individuals, and have identified how personal relationships develop and affect the work environment.

The next question is how do we prepare and create leaders for the future? After all, supervisors get promoted to mangers, leave for other organizations, or retire. At some point we will need to replace these individuals, but how do we prepare them to move the new leader to the move up next level?

The first, most important, is the need for education. While it is important to promote individuals with the best and/or experience, we need to educate and provide them with the tools to necessary to succeed at the next level.

Unfortunately, the promotion from staff member to supervisor, or manager, does not come with an instant knowledge of how to create a budget, plan for the future, or deal with personnel issues. Yet, this is often what we expect when the promotion occurs.

While some people are born with leadership skills, these traits need to be developed. First, and probably the most influential person, is the individual immediate supervisor. This might be the former supervisor, department manager, or any other person of influence in the organization.

In most cases, the individual selected is either the top performer in the department, or an individual that has the greatest seniority. Neither of these attributes prepares this person for the responsibilities and duties that are expected at the next level. This new leader is suddenly burdened with the responsibilities for the department budget, writing and reviewing policies and procedures, quality assurance, goal setting, and human relations issues.[49] [50]

In an effort to educate these new administrators numerous institutions offer "management" classes that teach the basics of the financial expectation, including presentations on how to create and manage a budget. This includes discussion of balance sheets, revenue and expenses, and profit and loss ratios. While this is great importance to the bottom line of the organization, it only prepares the new leader for one aspect of the position.

Given the expertise and experience from the individual's former role, they are usually well equipped to review the current policies and procedures of the department. However, this may also limit the new supervisor's ability to research and adopt new proposals to the current procedures. This is further hampered by the additional responsibilities accepted by the new leader. It becomes much easier to maintain the status quo, and "do things the way they have always been done". Instead of identifying and creating new solutions to old problems the department processes

---

49 Umiker's Management Skills for Health Care Supervisor. Charles R. McConnell. Jones and Bartlett. Ontario, New York. 2010. pp. 3-4.
50 The 7 Hidden Reasons Employees Leave: How to Recognize the Subtle Signs and Act Before It's Too Late. Leigh Branham. AMACOM. New York, N.Y. 2005.

become stagnant. New ideas that may stream line departmental processes are not identified and created, and the laboratory misses out on opportunities for growth and improvement.[51]

This same approach may occur with quality assurance and goal setting. Since the new administrator is accustomed to the techniques that they had performed, quality assurance often "looks like" the same program as the former supervisor. Again, this stifles growth and improvement.

Finally, the new supervisor has had little or no experience in resolving human relations issues, such as conflict resolution, employee motivation, and how to act as a role model for their employees.[52]

Interpersonal relationships play a large role in employee satisfaction, and how employees feel about their work environment.

The supervisor, given their daily interaction, and authority, over their peers plays a large role in creating the work environment.

Leaders that create an environment of display respect and caring build a positive work environment. When this occurs, there are high levels of employee morale and job satisfaction. As a result, these individuals provide improved customer service, which as described earlier, improves the financial performance of the organization.

If the new supervisor feels overwhelmed by the enormity of their new responsibilities it can affect their performance and how they interact with their employees.

The additional responsibilities of the new administrator may create a situation where they feel "pulled" in too many different directions. This creates a stressful situation and lead to frustration and poor performance. While the number of unfinished tasks may be of concern, it is more concerning how the new leader approaches and treats the personnel under their command.

---

51 Umiker's Management Skills for Health Care Supervisor. Charles R. McConnell. Jones and Bartlett. Ontario, New York. 2010. pp. 3-4.

52 Eichenberg, R., Lombardo, M. Twenty-two ways to Develop Leadership in Staff Managers. Part 4 of 4. GovLeaders.org. (1990). http://govleaders.org/22ways.htm

First, given the success they achieved at their former level, they start to expect their former co-workers to work perform to "standards which they had set". Due to the high level of performance they displayed, this often an unreasonable expectation. Not surprisingly, the inability of the staff to work at these performance levels leads to frustration on the part of the new supervisor and the former co-workers.

Second, since the performance of the department has suffered, the supervisor starts to feel a need to "manage" the department and co-workers. Instead of understanding that the highest performing employee has been promoted, the new administrator becomes frustrated that performance levels have suffered. When this occurs, the new supervisor becomes critical of the employees, and tries to "manage" the performance of the department and the employees. The attitudes of the employees deteriorate and the performance of the department suffers.

Another key issue is how the former co-workers feel about the advancement of "one of their own". Do they feel that the best person was promoted? Was there someone else who felt that they should have been picked? In these cases, the supervisor's manager must display support for the new supervisor, and help resolve these issues.[53]

Finally, some of these difficulties may be resolved by hiring a supervisor form outside the organization, or to place the department under another division.

In hiring an outside supervisor, the new leader should take time to appreciate the strengths and weaknesses of the existing structure. While it may be tempting to "dive in" and put new policies and procedures in place, one should understand how, and why, the policies of the department are written. Many times, the logistics of how things are done are a result of the resources available to the staff. In this case, it is important to ensure that new ideas will fit with the existing infrastructure. While change may be necessary, it is important to make sure that will also be effective.

---

53 Umiker's Management Skills for Health Care Supervisor. Charles R. McConnell. Jones and Bartlett. Ontario, New York. 2010. pp. 533-540.

Placing the department under another division presents similar obstacles.

To create an environment new leaders succeed, it is important that we identify and educate these individuals.[54]

Unfortunately, the promotion from staff member to supervisor, or manager, does not come with an instant knowledge of how to create a budget, plan for the future, or deal with personnel issues. Yet, this is often what we expect when the promotion occurs.

Prospective leaders should be identified in a process that is open to every member of your staff. Sometimes the best managers come from a person that you would least expect. In addition, an open process allows every team member an opportunity to advance and show their skills. Giving every member a chance at promotion reduces the frustration of privately choosing one person for advancement.

The process of developing leaders should be ongoing, and it will take time to complete the process. A comprehensive and complete process of identifying leaders to the actual advancement should be no less that one year, but less than two.

The ultimate goal should be to advance your team, and the individuals of the team, not necessarily to create a new leader.

By working through this process, you will find that not every employee is looking for promotion. In these cases, the individual is aware of the time and commitment necessary to step up to the next level, and are content in their current position. These individuals are often strong performers, and serve as part of the back bone of your department.

Next, good leaders are good role models. They know the goals and values of the department and the organization, and uphold and display those characteristics and traits. In addition, the employees watch the actions and behaviors of the leader, and will adopt those attitudes. If you are open and honest with them, they will respond in a similar manner.[55]

The development of new leaders should embrace these values. The goal of any program should be to improve performance,

---

54 Ibid.
55 Ibid. pp. 423-434.

team work, and reach common goals.Finally, building leaders involves improving your team. Leadership models involve every employee in the development of the team, and its policies and processes. This improves morale, rewards cooperation, and creates an environment where employees want to work.

While our table has three separate legs, the development of the organization, and the leaders that become managers should be an effort that reduces the gaps between the three supports.

When this occurs, customers, patients and employees all win.

CHAPTER 9

THE IMPORTANCE AND ROLES OF MENTORS

Some leaders are created, not born. They develop over a long period of time, and it is often necessary to have a mentor to fully develop their leadership skills.

Leaders are important because they are individuals that exceed company standards in performance, communication, customer service and teamwork. They are often self-motivated, observant and self-critical. They are constantly trying to improve their performance, and the performance of their unit.

While some individuals may display the characteristics of a leader, it is difficult, if not impossible, to fully develop these skills without a mentor.

A mentor is someone who has established themselves as leader and continued to develop their leadership skills. The role of a mentor is to share the ideas, knowledge and skills with their co-workers. They put in their skills in an effort to improve the processes and services that they and their team members provide.

To develop the next generation of leaders the mentor shares their knowledge, skills and expertise with the leader-candidate. Much of their influence comes from serving as a role model for their fellow employees. By displaying outstanding performance and service, they set an example, and share their knowledge with others to improve their efforts. More active efforts of the mentor, to the future leader, include discussing how to improve knowledge and skills, how to channel their energy in a more productive manner, how to conduct themselves with others, asking the right questions, and encouraging the student to ask questions.

In others words, leaders create more leaders.

Yet, good mentors are very difficult to find. A critical piece to developing a mentor individual is to create an environment in which learning is valued and rewarded.

Mentors, themselves start as leaders. Over time they demonstrate ideals such as outstanding performance, knowledge, communication skills and interpersonal skills. These individuals not only understand the basic skill sets to be successful, but they make an extra effort gain skills and knowledge that are not readily available. This is always involves learning form other leaders, including attending outside conferences, or learning different techniques and procedures. They hunger for learning.

Mentors are teachers and students. They are motivators and friends. They are individuals that work one-on-one with co-workers to develop the skills and knowledge that assist their co-workers to achieve greater success.

In addition to teaching skills, mentors are good listeners. They offer the leader-candidate constructive criticism and praise when necessary. They are involved in asking the right questions, as well as creating opportunities for the peer to develop and ask their own questions. They build a relationship with the leader-candidate and with co-workers. They make themselves available, and are quick to lightly praise the success of others. They display tolerance and, at the same time, provide discipline to reach desired goals.

An example of a mentoring situation occurs when students, and new graduates, learns to perform an echocardiogram. The performance of a sonogram is very technician dependent and requires extensive scanning skills and knowledge. The development of these skills requires extensive education, training, and practice.

An understanding of anatomy, probe positioning, and hemo-dynamics are essential in performing these examinations. While there are numerous technical schools that provide the minimum level of education, this is the only the beginning of learning and developing the knowledge and skills necessary to become a qual-ified sonographer.

During the educational process, in addition to the necessary class room education, it is essential that the student participates in a clinical setting. This includes working with an experienced sonographer that works with the student in applying the knowl-edge that has been gained from the class room.

I think that it is essential that an experienced technician actively participates in the training environment. This creates a mentoring situation.

The student, eager to learn the craft, is dependent upon the clinical leader to share the basic skills, and information, needed to complete a thorough and accurate examination. The experi-enced sonographer should actively participate in assisting the new technician perform the technical portion of the examination.

This type of situation provides an opportunity for mentoring. While the student has the technical knowledge of how the pro-cedure should be performed, and what information is gathered, there are numerous situations that require applications of differ-ent skills.

The windows, or areas that allow accurate images, are lim-ited in echocardiography by the ribs and the lungs. While sound transmission occurs in these structures, the sounds waves are distorted by these boundaries. As a result the sonographer must work between the lungs and ribs to appropriately image the heart. Further, in patients with lung disease, these windows are further limited.

As the anatomy of each patient is different, the ability to accurately record images the heart may require differing imaging techniques. Frequently the student will struggle to obtain the images that are required for a complete exam. In this case, a more experienced sonographer must be available to guide the new sonographer. At this level of support, the experienced sonographer is demonstrating leadership.

However, at some point during the training, the student's skill levels will reach a plateau. The student is performing echocardiograms on patients that have easily accessible windows, and this creates a level of satisfaction in their performance.

In order for the student to continue learning experience, is important that the experienced sonographer to keep challenging the new technician. This often creates a level of frustration on the part of the student, and the skilled sonographer must provide encouragement and support. This creates a mentoring relationship.

At this point, it sometimes becomes too difficult for the student and the experienced sonographer to continue the learning experience. The new technician has achieved a certain level of success, and does not understand how, why or when, a new technique may help them.

As an example, patients in that have a cracked rib may be unable to position themselves in an ideal location to allow the performance of the procedure. In this case, it becomes necessary to modify the technique to locate imaging windows to acquire an adequate exam. The sonographer has to change their technique, and, sometimes, accept suboptimal images. It is important that the new sonographer learns what images are acceptable.

At this point, in most instances, one of two situations occurs. Either one party gets so frustrated that the relationship, and the learning environment, suffers, or the mentor works with the prospective technician that both individuals and the learning flourish. In the first instance the student fails to continue to develop and their ability to learn new skills is severely hampered.

In the case of the mentor giving encouragement, the teaching environment will plateau, but the new sonographer quickly recovers and flourishes. The result is that there is a stronger bond between the student and mentor, and that the learning process becomes quicker. In addition, both the new sonographer and the experienced clinician display a newfound enthusiasm. Occasionally, the new student, or graduate will reach a plateau in the learning curve.

As an example, every patient has a different anatomical makeup, and the available acoustic "windows" may not be in a "normal" location. In these cases, an experienced sonographer would identify alternative "windows" that will allow a complete examination to be recorded..

At this point, the experienced technician needs to use the skills associated with mentoring. This would include showing the student where the locations where the alternative images may be acquired, and why they are necessary for that particular patient. In addition, the experienced echocardiographer should encourage the new sonographer to ask questions, should answer questions, and listen to the responses of the apprentice.

Additionally, as each person has unique personalities and learning capabilities, the environment, and teaching style, must be adapted the needs of the individual being trained.

Leadership and mentoring are embraced in the learning organization. These types of companies create environments and educational opportunities to assist in the development and behaviors which foster success.

While leaders create environments that encourage learning, mentoring is an active participation in the creation of these environments.

Like good leaders, good mentors are developed over time and effort.

CHAPTER 10

THE TEN COMMANDMENTS OF THE WORK ENVIRONMENT

The Ten Commandments of the work environment

I.) Thou shalt be respected, whilst respecting others.

II.) Thou shalt be treated in fair manner and treat other fairly.

III.) Thou shalt always respect the rights and needs of every person.

IV.) Thou shalt have right to a work environment that is free of distractions.

V.) Thou shalt appreciate that change is difficult, painful and necessary.

VI.) Thou shalt understand that errors are the symptoms of a larger problem, and not the problem itself.

VII.) Thou shalt understand that employees are part of the solution, not the problem.

VIII.) Thou shalt understand that while blame is easy, finding the right answers is hard.

IX.) Thou shalt understand that finding the best answer often requires everyone being involved.

X.) Thou shalt understand that while the customer comes first, they may not always be right.

Why do these commandments matter?

First, following these ideals reduce the number of distractions to the employee. These distractions may occur anywhere on the organizational chain of command. This holds true from the CEO down to the front line employees. If your employees are worried about how their supervisor treats them, this distracts them from properly performing their primary responsibilities.

Additionally, if the administrator feels like they need to watch every action of their workers, this distracts this individual from the duties and responsibilities of their position.

Whenever either of these situations occurs customers do not get the best service from the employee, and they often leave frustrated and upset. Not have you lost one customer, but they will share their stories with their family and friends, which affects the future business environment.

Another distraction that arises is when the administrator makes decisions that are neither fair nor equal. In an earlier chapter, we discussed an employee who was distracted by a supervisor who ignored a vacation request. The longer the situation went unresolved, the more uneasy the employee became. The end result was and the individual resigned from a department that was already lacking in staff members. This increases the pressure to perform on the co-workers, and results in sloppy performance by the remaining individuals.

Change happens. It is often difficult to accept, and is met by cries of "we've always done it this way". In the current business and regulatory climates, it is frequently necessary to adapt policies and practices. Individuals that have done the same job the same way for years are often unwilling, and sometimes unable, change to new thinking.

When this happens, it is necessary for the leader to adapt to the new requirements. New ways of thinking and operating must be developed. One answer to meet the new challenge is to involve the team members in creating new policies and procedures. In this way, you have an opportunity to review how the old processes need to be revised, why the new platforms are necessary, and how to get new and innovative ways to effectively integrate the new policies.[56]

Only incentive to involve the current employees is that is impossible for one person to understand the nuances of every process and available equipment. In addition, by eliciting their ideas, they take "ownership" of the processes and policies, and will adopt the new proposals more readily. By involving your staff in creating the changes, they will suggest ideas that maximize the effectiveness, and efficiency, of the processes in question.

It is easy to blame your employees. It is easy to identify a scapegoat. Often this is an employee that has "fallen out of favor" with the manager and is frequently found to be at fault. After several

---

56 Umiker's Management Skills for Health Care Supervisor. Charles R. McConnell. Jones and Bartlett. Ontario, New York. 2010. pp. 409-420.

events the employee works to minimum performance level so that they stay out of the manager's oversight. These employees are distracted by their perception, their performance suffers and they provide poor customer support.

In many of these instances, blaming the easiest perform or event avoids looking at a larger problem.[57]

As an example, in some of the clinical settings I have worked, the echocardiographer provides the reading cardiologist with a preliminary interpretation. This involves the technician reviewing the images to provide an accurate report. In cases when the images are not immediately available for review, the sonographer's impressions to the reading cardiologist may contain inaccurate information.

When this occurs, the reading cardiologist blames the technologist that performs the examination. While the sonography did, in fact, provide an inaccurate report, the true cause of the impression was the inability to properly review the images.

The correct course of action is to identify why the images were unavailable. Is the equipment malfunctioning? Was the computer system available to review the images? Was the sonographer busy and did not have adequate time to prepare? Was a limited study performed in order to address an immediate concern? Or, perhaps, there were time constraints for a competing procedure.

In any of these instances, the echocardiographer would not have been able to give an accurate technical impression.

Finally, there is the question of "the customer is always right".

In echocardiography, like many areas of health care, one size does not fit all. The images obtained on differing patients, and for different diagnoses, may require by utilizing differing maneuvers and positioning. In addition, many sonographers position themselves differently with regard to the patient. As examples, some sonographers scan form the patient's left, some on the right. While this may be a new procedure to the patient, the selection positioning allows the technician to perform their

---

57 Ibid. pp. 410-412

duties in a manner that is most familiar, and comfortable to the echocardiographer.[58]

In any profession, companies provide their employees' vacation time and sick leave. The importance of these benefits can not be understated.

Employees that are required to work long hours, and for extended periods of time, suffer from "burnout"[59]. The effects of burnout are a lack of focus, which results in making mistakes, decreased productivity, and poor customer service. They are quick to anger, and this is displayed in how they interact with co-workers and the patients that they are serving.

In health care there is the additional issue of the employee's responsibility to constantly address the illness and needs of their patients. Patients are stressed over concern over their infirmity, which may include issues of pain, the outcome of treatment protocols, and a desire to return to a state of normality. The individuals are dependent upon the health care provider for care and treatment. The caring and service that the physicians, nurses, technicians and support personnel provide compromises the ability to take care of their own mental health.

Thus, vacation time allows employee an opportunity to "de-stress" from the work environment. In addition, it allows this person to share time with family and friends, and gives them a break from the work environment.

Sick time allows the employee to deal with health issues, either themselves, or family members. Again, dealing with work and these health issues serve to distract individuals from their work, reduces focus on performance and productivity.

Similarly, an employee's superior may have a tremendous impact on the employee's performance. If the administrator is considerate of the needs of his constituents, then the employees will feel valued, and this will serve to elevate the worker's

---

58 Umiker's Management Skills for Health Care Supervisor. Charles R. McConnell. Jones and Bartlett. Ontario, New York. 2010. pp. 17-23.

59 Knowledge@Wharton (2006, November 15) More than job demands or personality, lack of organizational respect fuels employee burnout. (Online) May 13, 2011. http://knowledge.wharton.upenn.edu/article.cfm?articleid=1600

commitment to the supervisor and the organization. This improves employee morale, performance and customer service.

Individuals that work a 40 hour work week spend as much time at work, during the work week, than they do with their families. This puts a premium on their time away from the office, especially vacation time. Vacation time allows people to reconnect with their spouses, children, family and friends. When they return, they are often reinvigorated and ready to tackle their responsibilities.[60]

In the end this type of behavior affects every member of your team. As a manager, or a leader, you are judged by every decision you make. If you treat your employees' right, they will treat you right and will work to meet your customer's needs.

Ultimately, the Ten Commandments are about showing respect, concern and caring about your employees, productivity and ideas.

"If you want to be a better leader, be a better person".

---

60 Umiker's Management Skills for Health Care Supervisor. Charles R. McConnell. Jones and Bartlett. Ontario, New York. 2010. pp.533-540.

CPSIA information can be obtained at www.ICGtesting.com
Printed in the USA
LVOW101445020713

341213LV00018B/916/P